EARTH LIGHT

Peter Dale

EARTH LIGHT

Peter Dale

HIPPOPOTAMUS PRESS

ACKNOWLEDGEMENTS Versions of some of these poems first
appeared in the following magazines and publications: *Acumen; Agenda;
The Anglo-Welsh Review; The Big Little Poem Series; Chronicles
(U.S.A.); Le Courrier (Belgium); Elegies for Robinson Jeffers* edited by
Robert Zaller, Tor House Press (U.S.A.); *Exile (Canada); Footnotes;
London Magazine; Mandeville's Home Truths,* Mandeville Press;
*Outposts; Poetry Book Society Anthology 1986; Poetry Durham; Quarry
(Canada); Soho Miscellany* edited by Ian Hamilton, Bloomsbury
Publishing Ltd; *University of Toronto Review (Canada)*

The Hippopotamus Press gratefully acknowledges
the financial assistance of the Arts Council

First published 1991 by
HIPPOPOTAMUS PRESS
22 Whitewell Road, Frome, Somerset

British Library Cataloguing in Publication Data
Dale, Peter, 1938—
Earth Light.
I. Title
821.914

ISBN 0 904179 55 9
ISBN 0 904179 56 7 Pbk

*Ten copies of the cloth edition have been numbered
and signed by the author*

Printed in Great Britain by
The Starling Press Ltd., Rogerstone, Newport, Gwent.

CONTENTS

PORTENTS

Strangest things have been before,
    again, and mostly elsewhere:
sparrows will nest in a tractor—folklore
    the runes of geese on the air.

And our recounting them as rare
    bandies their wonder back to us...
and if the thrush we see is a fieldfare
    is the marvellous instance bogus?

And if, love, we both speak at once
    in the light of some other summer,
and say it is love, in all conscience,
    it has happened again somewhere.

Our shadows link hands in the wildflowers,
    gangling their length on the pathway,
and that chink-chink we hear as ours
    lights only once on this twayblade.

CRANE'S-BILL

Delicate misty bloom
    huddled away like your words,
a crane's-bill of powdery blue,
    mute for all its worth;

not to be gathered or pressed
    where it may grow again.
Let it grow here for the present
    we never took nor gave.

GIFTS

The thoughts I have I cannot give.
   I hardly bear them well myself.
Gifts of my hands I'd like to give
   and tell we share them here and now.

What the gift gives is what I'd give—
   behind this dumb, so yellow bloom...
I'd like to give you happiness,
   the cat that seldom comes when called.

OCCASIONS

I wasn't there to look
  the time you saw the lightning sear
the crooked oak.
  I had your fear for it.

I wasn't there the day
  you found a windcast blossom-shadow
spread from the may.
  Your joy I had for that.

—You let the bird go free.
  I couldn't see the blood that welled
but it seemed to me
  a bulb you held had burst...

When the love that I swear
  is a dry husk on the wind's breath,
I shan't be there.
  You'll have my death for it.

MINUTIAE

A petal of compacted mist,
you turn it in your hand,
my old miniaturist.
I shall never understand,
even in crisis, your openness
to moments of small delight;
unyielding, your hands caress
the porcelain, scalloped, white.

—So much of our time gone.
How I am watching you;
love, I am hanging on
that tinge of venous blue
where your inner wrist shows white,
and the porcelain gathers light.

WILLOW WALK

Willows cascade their curtains
over the towpath, into the water.
My legs go torpid; I cannot enter
    that tunnel.

The way you threw your tresses
over your forehead, into the basin,
your hands flurried, the trickles coursing
    the spine's runnel.

The blinking of an eyelid,
the shutter's action; there, at the outlet,
time, the axeman, with his mindless
    blade of light.

MEMENTO

What is this, you can't remember?
You have it pat if I forget.
You gave your word. The sun was amber,
setting. You know, by that gate.

So low it silvered drops of rain
beneath the bars. You reached your right
hand out to them, your fingers ran
them through and cross-marked the straight.

It's unbearable you can't remember.
The world's tears, woman. I was there.
That cliff of cloud, bruise-black and sombre
above the sunset's orange shore.

Some game! Forget the promise, love.
Recall the place that you swore on.
Yes, circumstantial—known as life...
We cannot go back there again.

Trapezoid shadow of the gate...
We used to try to change each other.
I can't believe that you'd forget.
When was that we gave it over?

VIOLETS

Oh, yes, you brought the violets in,
on to the kitchen sill,
to save them against the winter,
poor mangy things.

You and your green fingers.
But I know the drill.
You'll tell them, every spare minute,
of the summer they missed

that I never let you have.
And they'll parrot it back,
your smattering of a purple patch.
Everyone knows a chat

makes flowers of all sorts glad
to grow. You've got the knack.
What a summer we will have,
these winter annuals.

ANTIQUE

A silver candelabra, love?
Why on earth a candelabra?
Silver? Never in your life!

Or is it the olden days you're after:
a bit of tallow in an old tin?
Which of whose forebears lit a castle?

The twisted stems at every turn
reflect a tilted flame of lamp-light
a marriage of convenience, and tone!

But we can never light those candles.
Could we get back to last spring, love?
You leapt from my grasp, darted to paddle

your hands in the bluebells' haze, and the life
came back to you in that wild laughter,
at finding a pool the storm had left...

I've waited for you in the thick of darkness,
well-shaft to a pitch lid of water,
my head obstructing the only star-point...

Do not come back, my bluebell wader,
do not pull back from your dwindling pool,
once in living memory your wood...

Look, I have lit the candles. They pile
our quaking shadows over us.
Watch them. Watch as their tears spill.

GOLDENROD

More is forgotten than remembered.
  I cannot tell you why it is I hate
  these goldenrod. I've always hated them,
and any goldenrod, by any gateway.
  One day when I am old, and the glossed light
  of childhood seems eternity too late,
it may come back to me in living spite,
  prompting some feeling for an hour or spasm—
  dull, yellow-dusted peaks of even height—
when, deaf to me, the feigned enthusiasm
  of your vague words that never had a season
  is painless as passing time, the trembling aspen;
and love's become as trivial as these
  stalks of goldenrod, well out of it,
  that I smash and enjoy smashing as I please
because they have their season, and they split
  cleanly, unlike the pliancy of trees.
—Now match your forceful mouth to this mad fit.

FINDINGS

Finders are not keepers.
You found me as I was,
so you can skip that.
—Possession's just nine parts.

What I was needn't curb us,
though that is all you wish.
What I am will escape you
like the panache in your hat-box!

I am the bevel mirror—
breaking in three ways
the gold silence you admire—
ring, bracelet, hardware.

You warmed them today, tomorrow?
You lay them aside to wash.
But they leave a mark like marriage—
this allergy red raw.

—Ah, for your rheumatics,
a trace of gold to the wise!
The ring tightens its metal;
you'll hardly find it toxic!

Ring in the beak, magpie.
One is the sorrower's.
You will remember less smugly,
without a glint of respite...

Findings are for keepers.
As I found your taking ways
I keep them, the whole corpus,
scabs, allergies, pus.

VENUES

Take me through your old country,
even in words: mill out of function,
one chalky lane you never entered,
those summer evenings growing endless.

Show me, yes, the high pond, the branching
of the Sussex weed—that name once answered,
you're telling me you're told, for oak there—
over the two swans. I get the brochure.

Wrench me with options ours no longer
that the casual rich look vistas on to
and we admire... That lighted window,
stamp on a letter we shan't look into...

Turn to this meagre certitude, also:
my hands treading your inert torso,
swan's foot ivy on a stricken trunk,
paddling, liftless, to take the sun.

BRIC-A-BRAC

The glance of years ago,
  one forgotten afternoon,
you cannot now return, eyes slow,
  the gaze immune.

Okay, look around the room,
  old gifts, odd curios shelved;
silent, uninvolved, presume—
  your years undelved.

Clairvoyant to my days,
  you have the vantage over me.
Date my ivory, appraise
  this fake in memory:

a naked figurine, its style
  wide open, one for a pair,
Chelsea blue period, trial
  piece, none too rare.

Come in, do; and ring the bell,
  eyes immune, slow as that swan
in all-time junk. Pawn and sell,
  the antique con.

MIRRORS

The best and worst of us
   catch ourselves in a pose.
There, sprinting for a bus,
   already off the pace,
to some more sporting era—
or true self in the mirror?

The baton raised to beat,
   with hair and zip and flair;
the record turns, a sweet
   plush hush on the floor
of some melodious era—
or true self in the mirror?

Caught in the lamp-lit room
   beyond the window-pane,
the scholar who'll exhume
   the classic long-lost paean
of some more noble era—
or true self in the mirror?

Neat harp of the shoulder-blade,
   adze scoop down the neck,
Eve, is it, now portrayed,
   and naked as her nook
in that most perfect area—
or true self in the mirror?

Ah, barest one, is it you,
   self-mirror, self-admirer?
At other times, are you true?
   Is Paradise your era?
Or 'Mirror and the Sylph',
you're naked as yourself?

LIKE A VOW   A Sequence

LOCAL COLOUR

It feels like farewell to leave this area,
   as if to go would lose some thing of value,
though what it is I have no clear idea.

Not those cool harmonies, ochre and blue,
   these hessians, barley golds, the rusting bracken,
the Autumn scorches in the fields of fescue.

That pathway like a single wheelrut, then;
   redolent of somewhere that it wanders,
some journey long to rest, some friend forgotten?

No... nor the angled bough whose shadow stirs
   some element of dream across the moment.
Nothing to do with you, my love, nor others.

It holds no aura of the lost event,
   mine or the land's; no calm of mind; no trespass;
nor is there terror in it like a portent.

It's almost love that holds me to this space—
   despite a world I thought to leave at will—
in dread its power may rise in other places.

RECAPITULATION

A blade of cold water down the throat:
   huddle of trees and shrubs like green sheep...
the mill-pond brimming still as lead with threat...

And if with these unsummoned into shape
   they all are there and bound up with my head,
all days are there to rise with detail sharp,

can't I riffle to whichever day I had,
   and won't one show me what it is I want—
untouchable, exact and facet-hard,

as once I stared myself into a squint
   to catch, in the spouting barley-sugar-amber,
the skelter of the tealeaves as they went?

Nothing. But in the cup the usual number,
   dregs, always dregs—though grandmother at least
made fortunes of them as I now remember

one distant day when I was fearfully lost—
   wrong fork across the heath, not seen ahead
when coming from her cottage—time now glassed,

untouchable, enacted, period...
   And what the child would not, cannot know:
speedwell, red campion, in all likelihood.

So many lanes they waymark and renew
   that lead to nothing much that I would find:
speedwell, red campion, ragwort, I name them now.

They intervene, again have intervened,
   but those days passed as weeds some mood or itch
idly dispersed, or swinging jacket fanned.

Day! Where is the day I did not watch
   hands move, mind churn—its laughter free or feigned?
Merciless eye, that nothing can assuage!

UPLAND

I

A dry ditch, with banks of leafmould
  like wet rust, chestnuts overhanging;
a slate sky, contoured with sun-gold

above the horizon where a hamlet
  glistens. There will be rain, rain falling
big and warm and straight as a plummet,

splashing up coronets... Forgotten
  the hamlet's name, the last turning,
which next, but southern the location.

But I was on that upland; remember
  a pressure binding and releasing.
My memory haunts it like a spectre.

Perhaps it is the mind of others
  that leaguer there almost a feeling.
You would assume the wild-eyed watchers.

I find you many likely places.
  But if you're there you show no inkling.
You give them all your keenest glances

then off into the woods to savour
  the bluebells' well attested pooling—
ladies'-slippers found one summer.

But what is missing I cannot capture
  in trees, lane, ditch, the cloud purpling.
It is nothing that is in your nature.

But I am nearest it in silence:
  the sound of a bell no longer ringing.
It's almost like an old allegiance,

fealty sworn young to a lost lord.
  You cannot swear faith to my ghost-king.
I cannot breach his word, his gold-hoard...

Your bluebells, lass, this is your kingdom.
  In my lord's realm I'm the hireling.
Kneel to the bluebells, the blown blossom.

No once and future king, fore-spoken:
  his line will never see returning.
My oath can never be forsaken.

2

Lord, in the underlight of thunder—
  But if my liege is self-projection,
no ghostly exile of a lost order,

loyalty is no less though kingship
  is mine. What worse than king's treason?
I can't break faith by cant or gossip.

I say: no feint of trees and shadow.
  Not mine but earthly the dominion;
the bond is real as voice and echo...

No: beeches these; the promised shower
  small rain; and the wide sky ocean-
grey, not true to scarp and tenor.

But let it be: a part and parcel,
  our common ground of recollection,
the great, downsweeping branches focal.

(Curled husks of nuts like Dutch bonnets,
  the short-cut—geese in opposition,
a slate sky harrying high cloudlets

We used to eat the nuts when children,
   nails lifted by the shell's construction...)
Childhood, and the big rain not fallen.

3

Coronets of rain—and the keen-eyed
   child recalls their brief existence
sprung from the tarmac of the roadside.

And going up the narrow staircase,
   Candleman prancing like a nuisance,
coronets tumbled in a goose-chase

rolling down the gleaming rooftops...
   In the stillness of leaves and birds, the silence,
the weathered spirit senses raindrops,

knows the freshness that falls, releasing
   the tension, bringing out the fragrance
of the grass, the dry ditch jingling...

Trembler of light on its white column,
   coronets tumbling, dancing attendance,
Candleman, Candleman, once his kingdom.

But to your beeches as I know them,
   my scarp, how shall we plot our credence?
To know another takes a kingdom.

And the big rain is falling, watcher,
   the big drops in their regular cadence,
bigger than any tears, and warmer.

THE SUNKEN PATH

A land it was without companion.
No feature to detain the eye,
no sign of human cultivation.

I do not know how many times
I'd been there; have no recollection
of what event, which place nor why.

And yet it will not be forgotten:
the grass banks burred first left, then right,
like hammered pegs, the path so sunken.

Those weird birches, trunks awry,
the course that raindrops latch on
down a dirty pane—and the pines,

encroaching pines at the edge of vision.
The path wound up a steepish climb
toward a slate sky without motion.

Years ago, years, the lingering sight
but clearer, sharper the depiction...
It seems to lock into the mind.

*

But what holds over the hill-crest?
Do the pines' serrations meet
like jaws—a dark aquarial forest?

Was shelter once the driving need,
from bead-curtains of rain—or coolest
shade from the dusty August heat?

The path draws upward, still the clearest...
If you'd been walking there with me,
there would be something you had noticed,

a skipper, wildflower prove it real.
Your eye for small things always honest
to pin locality on a dream.

Show me the colour of bugloss, dearest,
fix it as somewhere you have been,
you with your eye for a wren's nest.

                    *

But which and where are the companions?
Are they long-barrowed by the tread,
this the landscape of extinctions?

In mind, I climb the likely bed
of winter rills, and the desertions
grow as congenial as a friend.

The path holds no commemorations.
Nor were you one to reach the head.
The air trembles with the derelictions.

There should be, just beyond the crest,
a church of leaning headstones, apparitions
of other people's, not my dead,

living times out of mind, deletions
of lichen, moss, the rain's fret,
but I, too, have made my exactions.

I have buried them before their death;
the living shall not haunt their perditions.
Love, the landscape seeps into my head.

*

—The boy stares long into the window,
watching a raindrop dither downward,
seeing another and another follow.

They're lit to silver at an awkward
juncture, to silver birch; the narrow
path meandering, pine bordered.

—Wenceslas footsteps, huge and hollow,
stilting the loose sand, striding upward,
those crumbling edges of sandgrains harrow

with the erratic stealth of rivered
drops on the pane that make an ox-bow
but always edging, inching earthward...

The horror of bubbles on the cocoa
bursting, the dry grains uncovered,
imprinting memory like a furrow.

*

Where are the friends of this madness?
Banish me from the lie of this land.
Love, show me the colour of bugloss.

GESTURE

Sand not discernible from sea,
   the sea not separable from sky,
mist like eroding promontory.

A girl zigzags the shingle, striding
   that drives her flaring yellow skirt
against her thighs, like a flame plying

from underneath a bough, exertion
   flapping her blonde hair from her shoulders—
a gale of her own with each diversion,

veering till mist obscures, then strolling
   clear a moment; she has no plan,
no firm direction that is holding.

—Blurring the foreland, rifted in canyons,
   encroaching combers that churn the stones—
mist and sea are her companions.

           *

That self-wind, mine. She plays the loner:
   hair and skirt, haphazard walk,
her pleasure in themselves, and donor

of mine, the emblems of a haughty
   sorrow, germane to mist and headland,
consoled by sea, the wave's exhaustion.

And to the life! It is the death
   of hope ... (Long live hope, the skirt knows;
long live hope, the blonde hair threshes.)

Pensive, perhaps, a child, she notes
　　the sand responding to her feet,
like skin against some grip or load.

And so it may be joy, the freedom
　　of lonely cove and lingering mist,
nonchalant gestures; none to read them.

　　　　　　　*

Mist and darkness obscure the figure...
　　A year ago? The gestures bloom
in streets and crowds, indelible vigour,

on hoardings, film—a casual beauty
　　or routine, but as the leaf runs true,
sorrow or joy, allusion, illusion...

Six feet of light between us and soon the
　　dark. I want to reach my hand
to touch your hand. It is the movement

of twenty years ago, this angle,
　　wandering like a stopped clock in time.
Love? It is the gesture. The candle

has not changed its spear of light;
　　my gnarled hand knows its root and branch.
A thousand shearwaters, one dive.

THE HILL
(In memoriam: R. C. Gray.)

I cannot do anything with this landscape,
    while you have settled down to see the views
and gaze across the valley to some mansion

sinking in green suds of trees—amusement
    enlivened for a moment by a train,
scaled to a model, that you find a nuisance.

I'd rather have it animate the ancient
    peace, I suppose it is, of field and covert;
but no hand will descend on it—extraneous—

and shift it to some tunnel. I have no love
    of miniatures, no god's yen for omniscience.
The aftermath is cut and stacked and covered.

And the path leads to stepping-stones; listen:
    the sluice of water that is water. Tears
would sound the same in volumes such as this.

There is no voice in the stream's whispered hearsay.
    There is no beauty here. It's all my eye.
See with the moth's light; catch the talon's fierceness.

Our tread erodes the path like the rain lying
    on the sun's scorched earth; soft or wild, the rain
that I'm attuned to more than any shining

of the sun—rain never visited with angels.
    And I remember once a day of downpours
when Bob, my friend—dead, in his strength, of brainstroke—

spread one oilskin upon the grass and, pounded
    by thunderous drops, both huddled, makeshift-tented,
under the other cape against the trouncing.

We had a grass-furred oilskin when it ended,
    and months before we'd plucked each blade or strand;
a talking point for years, our launching sentence ...

My eyes are locked through rain into this landscape,
    the stream and stepping-stones, the lucid shallows,
for my dead friend, and all of those whose handwork

is buried in each feature of the valley.
    Love, you shouldn't see it from this angle.

Hold still. A leaf's caught in your hair. Mallow?

RIVER

To hold in mind
these twisting paths,
this peace like the river winding.

How long will either keep
unblurred such peace
to flow on, sinewed, leaping?

That wren to be your emblem,
its jiffy poise,
pole-vaulter bending its stem?

Or these few speedwell mine
to make us pause,
return the river's winding?

But years, in distant years,
this time of peace
a drifting branch of hearsay?

That wren toppling a stem,
the speedwells' place?
Or like a vow remembered?

EVENINGS

Some reluctance to run away from sunset
and face the shadow's lank and teasing spleen.
A silence not ours but round us settled—
shrew to an owl, a kid's distant scream.

But half an ear we kept, paleface and redskin,
in fear and dread to hear them call our name.
Then lights, like afterthoughts, spread from one window;
the flame-chick flustered in the gas-lamp's cage.

Then in, to find them sitting in the hind-light;
darkness seeping from every edge and ledge
like water inching down a lock—recital
of all the highlights starring in our heads...

But they were looking over the dry brookside,
seeing a mist rise in the far fields,
and, like a fence, what heads above it riding,
watching the plectrum moon fail to appear...

And now we mull it over the old culvert,
the haze of London under blitz and fire,
watching the same moon fail to break the circle,
and, like an afterthought, put on the light.

RECREATION GROUND

"Did, Lily dear; did, Lily dear!" of electric told
the halves and quarters, not the pavilion clock;
and the steam freight huffed the time for home.
The bowling-green, a silent movie, rolled
as if slow-motion, under water; odd chock
and knock like some malfunctioned metronome.

The distant cries of games—they did not fade
but travelled off, always diminishing
as if forever right into the stars
and years away. Not an illusion made
by darkness edging in; that hollow ring
struck true...and truer now the railing bars

clatter across the carriage lights of a train...
I am reduced once more to a mute boy
gazing at the neolithic corpse
foetal in its museum pit again,
dreading not death but all the hoi polloi
that, unbeknown, will point with nosy gawps.

Terror, it gave, in any thoroughfare,
random as pigeons clogging up the ground,
stalk eyes that watch whichever way you tread...
And he curled in the great armchair,
eyes closed, to see how near would sound
the distant cries of life to the long dead.

Skin, like charred paper, bound his head.

SHAR

Expensive-seeming to a child,
your silverplate, Victorian frame,
Shar, promise of mysterious name,
my father's friend, you would be styled,
but uncle we were always told,
promised a visit there some day:
distinguished, fobchained, grey,
you looked more prosperous than old.

The promise holds my father gave,
old uncle Shar. I've come to you
a dozen times in sorting through
the double decade from his grave.
Today, I stop again, mid-chore,
depressed the frame is back in style;
compare this replica: a smile
of cousins, some Australian shore.

Your frame's fair dinkum, uncle Shar,
Victorian artwork coming home,
over-ornate, and made in chrome...
Your likely end's the school bazaar...
Old uncle Shar, I stare and stare,
the first time since that mantelshelf,
to penetrate into your self,
moustached, side-whiskered, debonair.

You'd be among the first to pack us
to weep and win the Falklands War,
Colonel Blimp and anti-Boer.—
Victoriana, the gone may attack us!
Old uncle Shar, my father's friend,
you'd ride a rhetoric like the hag's
and send us off with God and flags...
You kept your promise in the end.

Mine's the bazaar...
                    Tonight, I talked
of this and that, the nuclear end,
with you, their father's friend, my friend,
good wine and good wit you uncorked,
lover of women not so good
you always hoped, as their good looks;
of Marx, old wines, and older books;
and suddenly I understood:

my father, silent ironist,
he must have spelt it *Shah*—of Persia!
and kept the frame by some inertia.
How late it is to get his gist.
No visits now, old uncle Shah,
my father's friend. He could not bring
himself or us to Mafeking.
The empire of the dead's your spa.

THE OLD PATH

The path is there like an old friend
in a past one lives in more and more.
It would only take a letter, a morning.
A map would bring it all back fresh.
Through the spinney, round that coppice,
then the low fields, sheep cobbled.

Barbed wire and the fence posts cracked
across their tops like spider webs.
Seedheads of grass we used to wedge
in them in hopes they'd grow from scratch...
The one path that wandered undated
in childhood's single day.

How I remember it. Smith's farm.
Hazel withes after acorns, the clear light,
as if the essence of this life
we've had no need to share so far...
How well we corresponded, earlier!
You are dead now, gone to your earth.

But never mind the long silence.
I feel betrayed, and would betray
if I could bring myself to traipse
the path again, that stench of silage...

The moss on these posts. Do you remember
stroking the bumble-bees, my old messer?

THE WATER-SPLASH

The water-splash, you called it,
typical understatement.
A long time since I saw it.

But still in mind located
and you still on the high-point,
gazing long to savour it.

Dumb appreciation. Silence...
We knew we'd change, and thought
this, too, would be sanitised.

Our focal waterfall,
like an old English sheepdog
lolloping nowhere forwards.

He has no name or meaning,
but I have sent you this dog,
summers, as if you'd see it.

No telepathic responses;
your clear eye unflummoxed:
water and stone and mosses.

You and the falls a comfort,
while I have lost the place,
imagined every summer.

And on a heat-hazed day
I picture you on the slope,
and see the dog again.

Fetch him, boy! Fetch him home!
[Shoo him off and dismiss him
or you'll be soaked all over.]

I can't understand this distance.
How was it less than your death?
I'm not used to the difference...

And back comes old tousle-head
every summer into mind;
and the water-splash, as you had it.

PICTURE

I never loved her,
and you divorced her.
The downland vista,
that alto laughter.

Those hands that gather
her rope-tress spirals
so like two sparrows
that peck them together.

On a wooden stile,
she perches summer.
From where I am
a vibrancy still.

Old friend, it is
a faithful picture;
not a spectre,
nor duplicitous.

Those days were real.
If I recall her—
that high fan-collar—
it's no betrayal.

Friend, you betray
your biased eye.
And, sparrow, stay
in memory true.

The path was treed
with light-shuffled leaves.
The time of our lives
is all we betrayed.

STILL

Daughter, you are—if photograph
  may tell the truth without the eyes
  touching in shady velleities—
your grandmother's image and proof.

As was your mother—with the same if.
  From those old days: the untrammelled gaze;
  such carefreeness that never goes;
the lace but useless handkerchief.

—Speedwell after speedwell, path
  or hedge to tell each by her place
  and time, the trellises, the plush,
a future like a picnic heath.

It's more than mood, the hasty comb,
  blouse loose, unceremonious...
  I cannot swear to carefreeness,
but hope you may, in time to come.

Not as a grey nostalgiast
  but knowing what had been yourself.
  —Lass, must the held frame dissolve?
Both hold the present in the past?

Speed well, my only lass, speed well.

SUN

Dave, you were early dead
and, silly bugger, asked for it,
I'm afraid it must be said,
the way you drove. You must admit
it was the one thing you could do
to reconcile the world to you.

On this marvellous summer day
I remember you—not with tears,
affection, or regret I must say,
but pleased that after nine years
even with sods of your cut and run
death itself has not quite won.

CORRESPONDENCES

Letters as frequent as English rain,
   you have kept faith for twenty years,
   and faithfully that face appears
in mind, that shock of hair like grain
     before the scythe.

Don't tell me: you made the pub seethe
   hearing your plot to roast a swan...
   I now expect that marathon,
your six-mile trek in the blizzard's teeth
     to meet—by air.

Leaves under the closed door are
   lost voices in a foreign tongue.
   We scuffed them all about when young.
I've swept them up each year so far
     without fail.

Fall or Autumn, Autumn and Fall.
   And these rose-petals I gather
   make a wine that will not travel,
a scent and flavour I cannot file
     like an old address.

File this then in your legendries:
   this photo of a grey-haired idler
   (that doesn't really travel, either)
daydreaming into the autumn trees,
     willows and wyches.

And what you cannot see he watches:
   indolent swans on quiet waters,
   cupping, like hands, wings poised and faultless
to catch the light; and his half-wishes
     for that candid white.

COMMUNICATION (For Ian Hamilton)

Now miles and years have intervened,
do you, as I do yours, old friend,
still read my books? Would either read
them more if one of us were dead?
    And would a voice unearthed recall
    the years of silence that appal?

SOUVENIR

The very earth on which they stood
   is gone, three fists of withes,
poor pollards tilted at the wood's edge,
   reeds like scythes upended, crossed.

Beneath cloud slabbed with storm,
   their image skimmed with light...
Far friend, I hope with you a faded torment.
   Hindsight seems the last betrayal.

THE LINE

Leaves shoal the shores of lakes...
We confirm your instances,
nodding acquaintances,
old friends, with knowing looks.

Tortoise-shell shuts its blazon,
and gnomon-like it dozes;
across the lawn the daisies
succeed the cherry-blossom.

Your words have changed no tone.
Spine gold gone from the row;
gold dust in the slant ray,
and summer on the turn.

The soft riffling of leaves;
owl's hoot on the bare field,
black placemark in the fold,
the flicking of our lives.

Old friends, in the long shadows,
your cry goes through our head,
your cry goes through, still heard...
Is it the lamp that shudders?

LIFE-LINES

Runes, or the lines of life, as someone said,
and, like a palmist in reverse, I read them;
they come into my head, the vague and terse,
the odd flourish, freedom.

And something there about a father dead,
mark of an ungrateful son, love used—
so much unravelled thread, all said and done,
alias of the self-accused...

But, reading in your hand, the searing care:
a lifelong friend insane, a child dead,
the bonds of love that tear, I catch the pain
in all you wrote and said.

I leech into your sorrow again—forgive me,
living through all I read in your old slant...
In the dead season I live, old friend, I need
to be jealous of you, but can't.

BOOK MARK

A musty book of fusty verse,
deciduous dust of the old school room...
Someone has pressed a shepherd's purse
that tints the page with winter bloom.

Enlivened, I, poor fool of time,
flick to the bookplate for a claim,
and, wondering which had loved both rhyme
and flower, choose a faded name.

RIGHT OF REPLY

Dependable, the media don remarks
on the public words of private grief,
and reasserts his own belief
in the time-tried treason of the clerks.

—As if a drowning man whispered for breath,
as if a stabbed man stifled a cry!
The treason is, and is no lie
like his imagining your death.

PASTORAL

How though I stroke your flowing hair
this softly shall such gentleness
and love reach those in Bangladesh?
Or this preoccupied and scared
soothing of lines around your wrist
ease those who will not reach to age?
Your hands braid up your hair, touched grey.
Ah, love, I cannot cope with this.
Their shadows peck about the grit.
The least fall of a sparrow... The eye
is pummelled by their shadow wings.
The lilies of the field are blind.

THE LOST ONES
('Thy speech bewrayeth thee...'
                St Matthew, ch. 26, v.73)

The little girl had died at night...
I read of it in morning sun,
and two days after it was done;
I ought to take up pen and write...

(The mother never saw a line,
the culprit never read a verse,
no reader mourned behind the hearse;
what critics came to seek a sign?)

Little ones have died last night
in Bangladesh and Birmingham,
Morocco, Chad and Vietnam,
and all parts out of mind and sight.

(It would be honester by far
bewraying lilies of the field—
where they grow is bonemealed, bonemealed—
our little pretty ones they are.)

The little ones will die tonight.
Little ones die by Christ or Zen
and no blood runs from any pen...

And this is all I wrote tonight.

NEWSREEL

Among faces,
to recognise one I loved
would fix all in the mind,
but the eye refuses

the sweat of fear,
trenchings of tears and blood,
survival's grime,
blackening of fire;

they come, the faces
that might have been and were not.
Scan, don't improvise
resemblances or voices...

Depredation of years.
Love, we have made it. I turn
and meet your eye,
that poor, hurt face of yours

STEPS (A Woman is Speaking)

Ah, let him count my footsteps down the street!
As if he could, this quiet night of snow.
But only these two feet go down the flags...
And back again—wet pewter in the white.

I should have walked the unmarked roofs instead!
Daisies they look like, all those scrambled stars.
Soundlessly I tread; I'm like the snow.
This white will never tell me who I am.

No tally of my footsteps in this hush...
Tonight I'll pad up barefoot, soundlessly...
Back of a scrubbing brush, this dusty sole.
Strange with what narrowness we hold the ground.

A WOMAN SPEAKS TO GOD THE FATHER

Lord of the entire universe,
was there no one else to take?
No lively son in the womb's hearse,
no supple girl for you to break?

But you must take my dolphin man?
No boy to fall to you in play,
no white head broken like a fan,
no sinewed arm for you to fray?

Must I be jealous all my life
of six feet of claggy earth;
jealous of every trotting wife,
of every brat that's given birth?

I am jealous of you, God.
If I had every inch your might,
in my black hole you'd spoil your rod;
you'd kick up stars in endless night.

HOMAGE TO ROBINSON JEFFERS

You chose the bed by the sea window
                for a good deathbed
when you built the house.   You had it waiting,
letting only the odd guest sleep there,
not knowing its purpose,
yourself perhaps amused, as Death with you.

I don't know whether you died
                in that bed by the sea window.
I hope you did.   It is a small right,
like a birthright, the deathright
that we have betrayed like so much else
in this canned world that clutters the sea-rocks.

Your room that I have never seen
                I have always imagined,
rock-clean, relentless as your rhythm,
clear with dawnlight or the storm light,
noise of the great sea crashing beyond.
How I envy that clarity.

Wherever I reach my end, Jeffers,
                it will be in that sea room.
You whose words live on
have given me, unlike the Christ,
a place to die.

WILL

I'm an old man, shan't waste a word.
Never had much idea of the world;
and the one wish I had for you
never would have been much use.

I wish you liked books. Even my own
fool of a father used to hope
I'd love 'the good book'. (I went
over the top on that as well!)

Most of life is somewhere in a book;
more than anyone speaks, unboozed.
And mine went there, the whole shoot,
if you want to know me—not that you should.

Or could. Find me there when I'm dead,
in half a dozen books on a desk.
I'll be safe to know then, riffled,
as willows slide light into the river.

And the melancholy long shadows
will lean across the flickering shallows
and you may learn as the light lowers
only the dead heart is not alone.

MEMORIAL (For Frances Horovitz)

I never met you.
    The gut-reaction
to mourn your death is
    driven by anger
that time should wreck not
you as yourself but
as anyone else so
    circled with love,
    gentle with life.

Nothing I miss is
    you or yours to
wrench recognition.
    I cannot mourn you.
I'd have to give you
characteristics,
a touch, some charisma
    of others I love to
    feel your destruction.

Eleanor's hands,
    cool even in summer—
the image happens
    with such a sudden
shudder of anguish
and terror I am so
cold that I cannot
    touch myself. My
    hands mourn your death.

MIRRORS, WINDOWS

(A soliloquy: a middle-aged man observes his dead father's
features in his reflection in the window pane.)

A LIKENESS REFLECTS

Look at it, old face, in the window pane.
What do you think it feels? Thought you once knew:
timidity disguised beneath long patience;

weak humour an evasion playing neutral;
that everlasting hustle to escape
from any issue, household, local, nuclear?

—Tousled hairstyle, the voice's measured cadence,
those heavy spectacles... they hardly hide
the likeness. How have you come up to occasion?

But then it wasn't yours. (Who else with the hindsight?)
—You don't have to sit here and face this carping.
There you are, let that squirrel take the high-jump!

(Too many mirrors.) Spiral the trunk, scarper,
forelegs wide, back humped, a grand-prix car.

THE GARDEN BEYOND

A steady wind flows through the cherry tree;
along the topmost twigs aligns the leaves
like minnows swimming, motionless, upstream...

That low plank bridge across the bourn, a legion
of tiddlers holding station underneath;
those planks an ankle-width apart, unleashing

fears of legs in traps, a dread of kneeling
with all the rest.—Laughter without amnesty...
(Look away, face; true mirrors are amnesiac!)

Fear of water so deep it reaches to tears.
That inching down the face like insect duos.
—Dream of the leg bleeding ants, ants teeming.

Open the door. The rain will have to do
for this, child. Out, out. Open the door.

The bonehouse has no doors, and all the windows
reflect the images of self-defeat,
self-aggrandisement and self-acquittal.

Sit still. We'll flesh each other out, feature
for feature. Look on me, old man; as you used
to look; look on your son, feeling for feeling.

The long wait for triumph is over for you...
Not that gaze again, tacit and fixed.
You haunt weaker dead than living on my youth.

Silence consent? Or dumb déjà view? Fidget,
go on, give no answer. But do something.
Play with your pens, you've got a whole fistful.

Old man, look on him; look on your son
with that shiftless iron stare, that air presumptive.

REFLECTION REBUKES AND CHALLENGES

There is a time for speech, a time for silence.
Death gives most men but you the sense of it.
There was a time for words; you did not desire them.

What the headstone speaks the living issue.
The dead shall not come to living beck and call.
You never heard me speak, not a single instance.

Ventriloquise me now from your little corner.
Speak to your son. (The pane stares back at you.)
Your son, not me. Time for the wise and cautious.

Ventriloquise me now! Here's to reunion!
And I shall tell if you talk in character.
I shall reflect on his and your ill-usage.

Ventriloquise me: muggins, the taciturn.
(Who says does not know. But you're determined.)

THE GARDEN BEYOND AND BEYOND

The minnow leaves have made no sign of headway,
flickering like light tethered in the current...
What water, sprats of sun, when Bob, quite helpless,

flashed skidding through the ford, one dry escutcheon
where saddle saved his seat...
                              A sort of shining.
Like couchgrass heads the gutter ripples scurry.

—The gold nib gleamed and buckled with my shying.
It was that day of grief my mother died.
I watch it crumple. Sorrow? Selfish icon,

my first fountain-pen, or true digraph?...
Under the table with the torch-light dimming,
waiting for dark to hone the beam, motes diving

and soaring in the shaft. I watch them dither,
drifting out into night. (Moth, you are dizzy.)

WISE AND CAUTIOUS

Son, I cannot tell you how to live.
The lightning lasts a flashy second's worth.
Rock can't keep the spate inside its limits.

Oak cracks in storm; but mouths may keep their word.
I promise nothing; we shall miscomprehend
each other and possibly do much worse.

Yet do not look on this in long years hence
and blame yourself for every misconception,
nor grieve when I am gone upon this head.

Promise me nothing; vows are sworn to the self:
make sure the word you give will wear like diamond.
(And one other thing: get yourself an obsession.)

Son, I cannot tell you how to die.
So do not watch me. No date for your diary.

REFLECTION HECKLES

That's not very knowing. What do you say?

My words are silent. Silence that is golden.
(Slaves of the crucified deserve the same

in image of the only (mis)begotten.
You couldn't manage that, so had to sham
self-martyrdom, all those petty golgothas...)

Not even the sun is enough. We are shadows
of flames and risk becoming shadows of bombs.
Twice a day the brilliant sun can shackle

our hindleg stance to its stalking bondage,
the squat tortoise at noon, the gangling hank
at sunset. We have parodied the body

of the dog, the cat, the horse but never hatched
so many creatures fashioned without hands.

COLLOQUY

A handyman, is it, now? And what can hands
do more than minds about it? Pull the curtains?
Fidget with pens? Settle a tinkers' haggle?

—Your hand, man, from the grave, and in my cursive
so studiously unlike yours, old bible ham;
give me your hand, conclude this running skirmish.

Give me your hand; you never gave me a hand.

—The dead can't plead for those that live and suffer;
the living may not pray for the dead. The has been

is forever has been. Advise your son
while he is still alive. Put him wise.
Feed experience to his wide presumption.

Trust you to put it straight in black and white.
—Or the old block will know the reason why.

HE ADDRESSES HIMSELF TO REFLECTION

The minnow leaves have made no headway yet.
The only way is down, for all their darting,
and they, like you, go down without a yelp...

Father, father, no more; the glass is dark.
I've put the light out. Now the moths have gone.
You've never haunted darkness, poor cadaver.

You're laid to rest. I give my word as gospel...
I suppose I'll watch the leaves, the squirrel
a few more years, still heckle autumn's gossip,

sometimes catch your tones. I cannot acquit you.
And this abeyance gives no satisfaction.
Lie easy as ever—and forgive this quibble.

Years, years spent pouring words we couldn't fathom.
Only through death we speak in honest fashion.

VENTRILOQUY

My son, you haunt me with my hasty youth.
The genes have won! And nothing I have tried
has saved you from the worst, or been much use.

You look at me as I have stared in triumph
over my father, seeing what only seemed
incomprehension, suffering his casual triteness.

I don't much like the glare of your conceit.
I've lived your mood. You haven't reached my mood
or feeling, history or hope, season for season...

If you look, there is a blue tinge to the moon.
Sliver of apple on the knife... My voyage
is almost over; your promontory is moving.

—Who's speaking, please? Father, is this your voice?
Late, so late. The line is dead. Void, void.

NOTES

Willow Walk   (p. 14)

The word 'forehead', in verse 2, in my pronunciation rhymes with 'horrid'.

Like a Vow   (p. 23)

I am indebted to the following friends who read this sequence and made valuable suggestions: Humphrey Clucas, Kevin Crossley-Holland, Kenneth Crowhurst and Roland John.

The Sunken Path   (p. 30)

v. 8, 1.2. I pronounce the word 'lichen' like 'liken'.

Shar   (p. 39)

In verse 4, and line:
    Victoriana, the gone may attack us
is a parody of a line from the jingoistic ballade *A Ballad to Queen Elizabeth (Of the Spanish Armada)* by Austin Dobson:
    Gloriana! The Don may attack us...

In the last verse, the town-name Mafeking (now Mafikeng) is intended to remind of the verb 'to maffick'—recorded as archaic nowadays—which meant exaggerated jingoistic rejoicings as occasioned by the raising of its siege in the Boer Wars.

A Woman Speaks to God the Father   (p. 58)

This poem turned up verbatim in a dream. The only waking change I had to make was to replace 'perpetual' with 'endless' in the last line for rhythmical purposes.

Mirrors, Windows

The Garden Beyond and Beyond   (p. 66)

11.3-6. These somewhat cryptic lines refer to a friend's crossing a ford at speed on a bicycle so that only the part of his shorts on the saddle remained dry—one of those random memories that stick in mind seemingly the touchstone of something significant.

1.7. Just after the Second World War, fountain-pens were expensive objects not lightly given to children. Torches were magical toys also, after the war years of eking every last amp out of more or less flat batteries.